No hand cranking! No electricity! No salt! With a Donvier, you have ice cream in less than 20 minutes. But just to remind you of what it used to be like, our 83 thoroughly modern recipes are set in an album of pictures from the past.

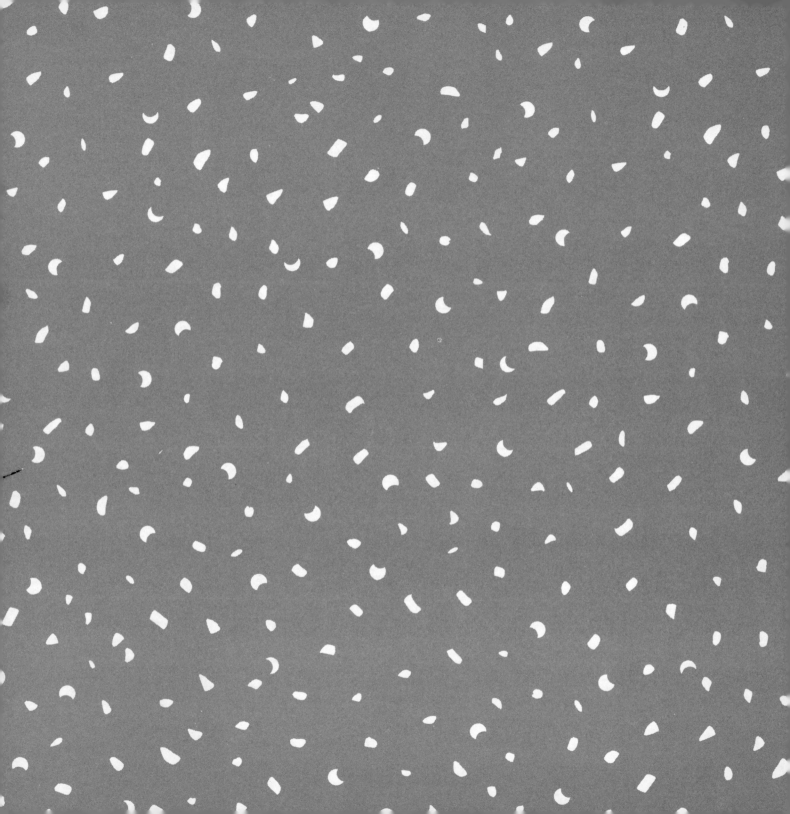

Ice Cream

*Created For
Donvier By
Irena Chalmers
& Friends*

*Recipes Tested By
Peter Kump's New York Cooking School*

PENGUIN BOOKS

PENGUIN BOOKS

Viking Penguin Inc., 40 West 23rd Street
New York, New York 10010, U.S.A.

Penguin Books Ltd, Harmondsworth
Middlesex, England

Penguin Books Australia Ltd, Ringwood
Victoria, Australia

Penguin Books Canada Limited
2801 John Street
Markham, Ontario, Canada L3R 1B4

Penguin Books (N.Z.) Ltd
182–190 Wairau Road
Auckland 10, New Zealand

First published in the United States
of America by Irena Chalmers
Cookbooks Inc. 1986

Published in Penguin Books 1987

Printed in Baltimore, Maryland
by John D. Lucas Printing Company

Donvier® is a registered trademark
of Nikkal Industries, Ltd.

Editor Helen Scott-Harman
Interior Art Direction & Design Karen Skelton
Production Assistant Rebecca Trahan
Picture Research Carousel Inc.

Photo credits appear on page 94

CIP data available
ISBN 0 14 01.0237 X
Library of Congress Catalog Card Number: 86-40554

❧ Contents ❧

Introduction

W ay back in the glorious days of yesteryear, there were a few things in life that were very, very glorious—such as homemade ice cream, for a notable example—and there were some other things that were decidedly LESS than glorious, or glamorous, or amorous, or even remotely amusing—such as trudging out to the kitchen and making it.

The dream that gave rise to the scream was legitimate enough, and universal on summer days when everybody was collapsed on the porch, fanning themselves to beat sixty. But the job itself usually fell to the poor soul who voiced the idea in the first place—who else was going to climb down off the chaise voluntarily and run around in all that heat?

The poor soul's first task was The Assembling of the Elements. The ice cream machine was, of course, put away tidily down in the cellar somewhere out of the way and out of mind. Give the poor soul an hour to find the machine. As for the ingredients, there was always plenty of cream and sugar, milk and eggs in the house, and of course, the vanilla. But would there be enough ice in the ice box? No. And when would the ice man be calling again? Next Tuesday, you say? So there was nothing for it but that the poor soul would have to hasten down to the ice house to buy a nice big block of ice—the ice man would fetch it out to him with a huge pair of tongs—and the poor soul would hasten home with it, dripping, and then take an ice pick and hack it to bits, risking puncture wounds with every frantic blow to the unyielding cube. The poor soul would have to find a towel to wrap around his hand, the better to protect himself from the blade-sharp shards of ice.

When the poor soul had reduced the ice block to a pile of slippery, spiny chips, he had to pack them into the machine's casing, together with a liberal dose of salt. SALT? Yes, rock salt. Is there any rock salt in the house? Gee. Time for another trip down to the cellar. Where else to find rock salt on a Sunday afternoon in—shall we say?—1935.

Let's say he found the rock salt, and by now, everything was ready. Well, not exactly everything. The ingredients had to be cooked into a custard and then chilled. CHILLED! Yes, so the mixture wouldn't melt the ice in the machine. But how? These were days before there was a refrigerator in every kitchen; far from. If there was an ice box, the poor soul could sit the mixture on top of the ice block in the ice chest and fan it cool. One ingenious solution was to dig a hole in the most shadowy part of the garden, if you HAD a garden, and bury the covered mixture in soft loam.

When all was in readiness, the poor soul poured the mixture into the belly of the machine, put the plunger and the dasher in place, and commenced to crank. And crank. And crank. By now the day had turned to dusk, and the family was *really* screaming for ice cream, and the poor soul cranked away for all he was worth, while everyone wondered aloud what all the fuss was, and wondered aloud just how long it OUGHT to take for a family to have a little taste of ice cream, after all.

Finally they all sat down on the porch in the gloaming, contentedly spooning up their dollops of wonderfully delicious soft ice cream that was melting in their plates, thinking nice thoughts about how nice it was for the family to be together, maybe even thinking nice thoughts

doubtedly was enjoying HIS
thusiastically than anybody

on't do it that way anymore.
h enables us to make ice
minutes. And this book of
make all kinds of icy treats
nk or a trudge to the ice
at no one will pity you, or call
you a poor soul, when you produce lavish and delicious
icy treats from your own kitchen. Instead, they'll call you
smart; and after all, what's more rewarding: pity, or
admiration?

Your Donvier is not, of course, just for making ice
cream. It's for sherbet and sorbet and ice milk and ices
and sundaes and frozen desserts, with flavors inter-
mingled with flavors, and with fresh berries and fruits,
and nuts and sprinkles, and crushed M&Ms and broken-
up Heath bars, and a myriad other combinations as far
as the mind will stretch.

As for cold drinks, it will chill a margarita or a tall
glass of lemonade. It will give you a tumbler of iced tea
without diluting the taste with ice cubes. It will cool the
Vichyssoise, or any other cold soup—cucumber,
avocado, cherry; and it will chill a couple of splits of
champagne or a half bottle of wine.

The Donvier has joined the food processor and the
microwave oven in radically changing the way we
live today by radically reducing the amount of time
and labor it costs to eat not only well but lusciously.

Persons of good taste have always screamed for ice
cream, cold soups and frozen desserts. When the
Emperors of Rome screamed for that kind of thing,
minions ran relays forth and back to the Alps to fetch
buckets of snow from the mountaintops. In the 1920s
and 30s, the poor soul worked half the day to oblige his
family with a cool summer treat.

Today we live a very different way—thanks to
Donvier.

♥ IRENA CHALMERS

Dear Reader,

*All the recipes in this book were carefully tested during the summer months when most fruits are
at the peak of their season and bursting with fresh, sparkling flavor. You will readily recognize that
during July and August the peaches, strawberries and other fruits are more juicy than at other times
of the year. We ask you to bear this in mind if you are making your own ice cream and sorbets when
the snow is on the ground, as there will inevitably be some slight variation both in the intensity of
taste and in the ultimate quantity yielded from the recipe. A spoonful of preserves will do wonders
to brighten the taste of the fruit. But do be cautious about adding more than tablespoon of fruit-
flavored brandy to the mixture as too much alcohol will prevent the ice cream from freezing.*

*Note: All the recipes that follow have been given for the pint-sized Donvier. They can safely be
doubled or halved to fit the other sizes in the Donvier family of ice cream makers.* ♥

Instructions

1. Turn your freezer dial to "high." The ice cream maker will not work on "low." Set the freezer temperature at −18 degrees Centigrade (0 degrees Fahrenheit).

2. Remove your assembled Donvier from the box and disassemble it, removing the Chillfast aluminum cylinder from the plastic outer case. Wipe the inside of the cylinder with a clean dry cloth. For air-cooled freezers: Place the cylinder, with the plastic ring attached, open-end up in front of the cold air vent in the back of the freezer. For direct cooling type freezers: Place the cylinder upright on the floor of the freezer. Do not place it upside down or on its side.

3. Leave the cylinder in the freezer overnight—for at least 7 hours.

4. Take the thoroughly frozen cylinder out of the freezer.

5. Place the frozen cylinder in the outer case, aligning the triangle marks on the ring and the case.

6. Fit the bottom of the blade into the bottom of the cylinder.

7. Immediately pour the prepared mixture into the frozen cylinder. Quickly place the lid on top, fitting the center hole directly over the top of the blade.

8. Quickly attach the handle and turn it clockwise 2 times every 3 minutes. Continue this procedure for 15 to 20 minutes. It is not necessary to turn continuously—let Donvier do the work. When the steady freezing of the ingredients makes turning difficult, turn it in the opposite direction. Freeze the ice cream to the desired consistency.

9. When you have finished enjoying your homemade ice cream, wash and thoroughly dry the Chillfast aluminum cylinder.

Storing the cylinder in your freezer insures delicious ice cream at a moment's notice, whenever you feel like it.

Helpful Hints For Making Ice Cream

1. Make cooked ice cream bases at least one day ahead. This allows them time to cool properly and the volume will be maximized. Pre-chilling of each base is recommended!

2. If only yolks are called for in a recipe, use the whites for other recipes included here, or use them to make baked meringue shells to serve ice cream in.

3. If only egg whites are used in a recipe, as in some sherbets, save the yolks for cooked bases that call only for yolks, or add them to enrich other cooked bases.

4. Richer, creamier ice creams can be made by adding more cream and less milk.

5. Lighter ice creams can be made by using more milk than cream, or by eliminating the cream altogether. Most recipes will work if skimmed milk is used, although there will be a change in texture.

6. Uncooked ice creams will give best results if you use an electric mixer to "cream" the eggs and sugar (or honey). This maximizes the volume and helps incorporate the sugar into the mixture.

7. Because alcohol added to ice cream results in a softer texture, you may wish to add this later in the freezing process rather than at the beginning.

8. All ice cream mixtures should keep well for 2 to 3 days in your refrigerator. Just pour into the frozen Donvier when you are ready to use.

9. Acidic ingredients (including almost all fruits) should be mixed and stored in non-metallic containers as metals may cause color or flavor changes.

10. When pouring the ice cream base into the frozen cylinder, stop half an inch from the top to allow the ice cream to increase in volume during freezing.

11. To avoid damage to the aluminum cylinder, use only a rubber or plastic scraper or a wooden spoon to remove its contents.

12. Ice cream made in the Donvier will have a soft, smooth texture. For a firmer texture, simply remove the blade and replace the lid and cap, and allow it to sit for 30 minutes.

13. Water-based frozen treats, such as sherbets, juices and sorbets, require more frequent turning of the blade. Just turn every minute or two for a smooth freeze.

14. In the unlikely event any ice cream is left over, you can store it in a plastic container in the freezer.

Caring For Your Donvier

CARE AND CLEANING

1. After using, wash the freezer cylinder with a sponge or soft cloth in lukewarm water with a mild detergent.
2. Rinse completely.
3. Wipe the cylinder thoroughly dry.
4. Store in a dry place or *keep in the freezer*.
   Note: The Chillfast refrigerant used in the Donvier cylinder is absolutely non-toxic and safe.

SOME DON'TS

♥ Never wash the freezer cylinder in the dishwasher.
♥ Never use a scouring pad on any part of your Donvier.
♥ Never wipe the plastic parts with cleaning solvents.
♥ Never heat the freezer cylinder in any way.
♥ Never handle the frozen cylinder with wet hands.
♥ Never freeze the plastic parts of your Donvier. Always remove the blade, lid and handle before placing the Chillfast aluminum cylinder in the freezer.
♥ **Never allow children to use the Donvier without supervision.**

VARIOUS USES FOR YOUR DONVIER

Ice pail: Just remove the handle and the blade, and insert the cap into the hole of the lid. Ice keeps for 3 hours.

Quick cooler for iced coffee, tea or soup: Hot liquids can be cooled instantly in the frozen cylinder.

Ice cup: Pour water into the frozen Donvier cylinder and you'll have a perfect ice cup in about an hour.

WHAT WENT WRONG?

If you did not get what you expected, one of these might be the reason:

1. The cylinder was not completely frozen.
♥ The cylinder was placed too near the freezer door.
♥ Food items blocked off the cold air vent in the back of the freezer.
♥ The cylinder was placed on its side.
♥ The cylinder was left in the case or with the cover on. (Never cover it with anything.)
♥ In direct cooling type refrigeration, the entire freezer interior may have been frosty.
♥ The cylinder may have been left at room temperature for more than 10 minutes after removing from the freezer.
♥ The cylinder may have been in the freezer for less than 7 hours.
2. The ingredients were warmer than room temperature.
3. The volume of ingredients exceeded the maximum capacity as specified in the recipe.

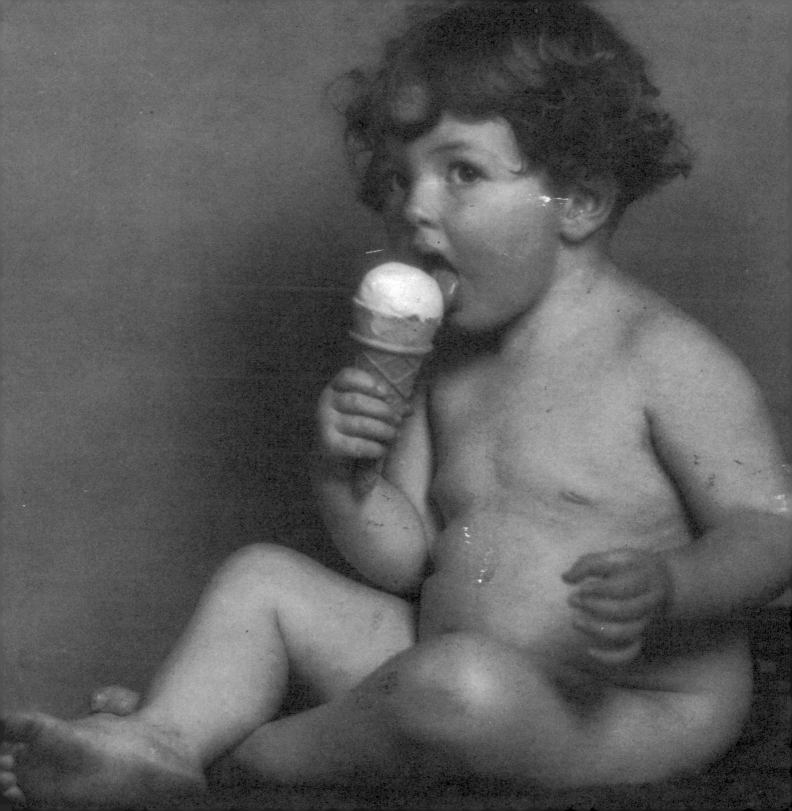

Ice
Creams

Much of the pleasure of the Donvier comes from the fact that you no sooner begin to think you would like to have some homemade ice cream than there it is—in less than half an hour. If you are having a little roast chicken for dinner and you have your Donvier cylinder stored in the freezer, you can start the ice cream and by the time the chicken has cooked, the ice cream will be frozen and ready to eat.

If you store homemade ice cream in the freezer for several days, however, it will become quite hard because it does not contain all the emulsifiers and stabilizers and chemicals that are found in commercially made ice cream. To soften it slightly, place the ice cream in its storage container in the refrigerator for 30 minutes or so.

If you don't expect to be eating the entire quantity that you have made immediately, the addition of a lightly beaten egg white or a tablespoon of white corn syrup will help to keep it smooth and not too firm. ♥

Vanilla Ice Cream

Sometimes the simplest things are best, like this Philadelphia-style vanilla ice cream.

Makes about 1 pint; recipe can be doubled for about 1 quart.

1 cup milk
1 cup heavy cream
⅓ cup superfine sugar
1 teaspoon vanilla
  extract

Combine the milk and cream with the sugar. Whisk for about 2 minutes, or until the sugar dissolves. Stir in the vanilla extract. Chill if necessary.

Freeze in your Donvier Ice Cream Maker according to the instructions on page 10 .

Peach Ice Cream

Few things bring so much joy to the soul as a bowl of sliced peaches crowned with a very large scoop, or two, of freshly made peach ice cream.

Makes about 1 pint; recipe can be doubled for about 1 quart.

3 medium-size ripe
  peaches, 2 of them
  peeled, pitted and
  sliced; remaining
  1 peach peeled,
  pitted and very
  finely chopped
½ cup milk
½ cup heavy cream
⅓ cup superfine sugar
1 teaspoon vanilla
  extract

Puree the peach slices in a blender or food processor. Refrigerate.

Combine the milk and cream with the sugar. Whisk for about 2 minutes, or until the sugar dissolves.

Stir in the vanilla extract. Add the peach puree, stirring well. Chill if necessary.

Freeze in your Donvier Ice Cream Maker according to the instructions on page 10 , but remove the blade a few minutes sooner and stir in the chopped peaches. Proceed as directed.

♥ LITE VERSION

For Peach Ice Milk, substitute low-fat milk for the milk and whole milk for the cream; and reduce the amount of sugar to 1 tablespoon.

Strawberry Ice Cream

When the strawberries are exploding with summer-ripe taste and sweetness, you will unhesitatingly make ice cream with the fresh berries. On a cold winter night, though, you can whip up a batch of homemade ice cream using frozen berries (although if the package says it is packed in syrup, there has been sugar added, so reduce the sugar in the recipe accordingly).

Makes about 1 pint; recipe can be doubled for about 1 quart.

½ pint fresh straw-
berries, or half of a
10-ounce package
frozen strawberries
¾ cup milk
¾ cup heavy cream
⅓ cup superfine sugar
1 teaspoon vanilla
extract

Rinse and then hull the fresh berries. Puree them in a blender or food processor. Strain if desired. Refrigerate.

Combine the milk and cream with the sugar. Whisk for about 2 minutes, or until the sugar dissolves.

Stir in the vanilla extract and the pureed strawberries. Chill if necessary.

Freeze in your Donvier Ice Cream Maker according to the instructions on page 10 .

♥ **LITE VERSION**

For Strawberry Ice Milk, substitute low-fat milk for the milk and whole milk for the cream; and reduce the amount of sugar to 1 tablespoon.

Pistachio Ice Cream

The pistachio nuts for this ice cream should be the widely available pre-roasted kind. You can use either salted or unsalted ones; salted pistachios give the ice cream's flavor more complexity.

Makes about 1 pint; recipe can be doubled for about 1 quart.

¾ cup milk
¾ cup heavy cream
⅓ cup superfine sugar
¼ teaspoon almond
extract
⅓ cup shelled, chopped
pistachio nuts

Combine the milk and cream with the sugar. Whisk for about 2 minutes, or until the sugar dissolves.

Stir in the almond extract and the chopped pistachio nuts. Chill if necessary.

Freeze in your Donvier Ice Cream Maker according to the instructions on page 10.

♥ **LITE VERSION**

For Pistachio Ice Milk, substitute low-fat milk for the milk and whole milk for the cream; and reduce the amount of sugar to 1 tablespoon.

Chocolate-Almond Ice Cream

A fine dessert to have with a mug of hot chocolate in the winter—or to serve with some chocolate cookies any time.

Makes about 1 pint; recipe can be doubled for about 1 quart.

¾ cup milk
¾ cup heavy cream
⅓ cup superfine sugar
1 teaspoon vanilla extract
15 chocolate-covered almonds, chopped

Combine the milk and cream with the sugar. Whisk for about 2 minutes, or until the sugar dissolves.

Stir in the vanilla extract, then stir in the chopped chocolate-covered almonds. Chill if necessary.

Freeze in your Donvier Ice Cream Maker according to the instructions on page 10.

♥ LITE VERSION

For Chocolate-Almond Ice Milk, substitute low-fat milk for the milk and whole milk for the cream; and reduce the amount of sugar to 1 tablespoon.

Peppermint Ice Cream

For a variation, try adding 3 ounces melted bittersweet chocolate, to make Chocolate Peppermint Ice Cream.

Makes about 1 pint; recipe can be doubled for about 1 quart.

6 hard peppermint candies
¾ cup milk
¾ cup heavy cream
⅓ cup superfine sugar
1 teaspoon vanilla extract

Crush the peppermint candies between sheets of wax paper with a rolling pin.

Combine the milk and cream with the sugar. Whisk for about 2 minutes, or until the sugar dissolves.

Stir in the vanilla extract and the crushed peppermints. Chill if necessary.

Freeze in your Donvier Ice Cream Maker according to the instructions on page 10.

♥ LITE VERSION

For Peppermint Ice Milk, substitute low-fat milk for the milk and whole milk for the cream; and reduce the amount of sugar to 1 tablespoon.

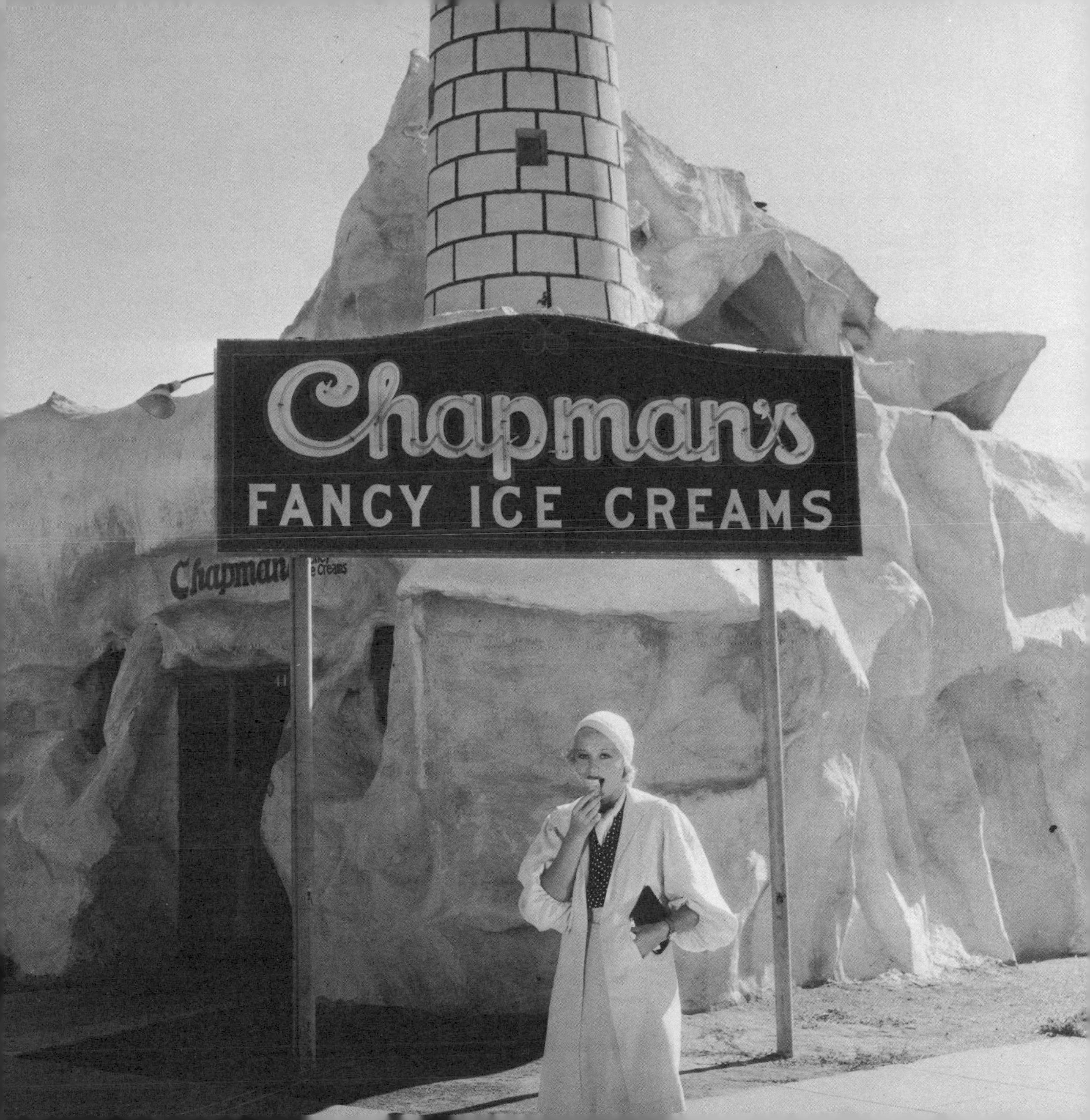
Chapman's
FANCY ICE CREAMS
Chapman

Lemon Ice Cream

The lemon's sharpness is cushioned in soft cream—a beautiful contrast and a superb ice cream. It is particularly good served with a bowl of blueberries.

Makes about 1 pint; recipe can be doubled for about 1 quart.

1 cup heavy cream
½ cup milk
½ cup superfine sugar
½ cup strained fresh
    lemon juice (about
    3 lemons)
Grated rind of 3 lemons
1 teaspoon vanilla
    extract

Combine the cream and milk with the sugar. Whisk for about 2 minutes, or until the sugar dissolves. Stir in the remaining ingredients. Chill if necessary.

Freeze in your Donvier Ice Cream Maker according to the instructions on page 10 .

Mango Ice Cream à la Diana Kennedy

The foremost authority on Mexican food, even in the view of the Mexican government, is the formidable Englishwoman Diana Kennedy. For her most personal cookbook, Nothing Fancy, *she developed the exciting recipe that inspired this adaptation.*

Makes about 1 pint; recipe can be doubled for about 1 quart.

1½ medium-size ripe
    mangoes (about
    1½ pounds)
1 tablespoon lime juice
2 tablespoons light
    brown sugar
3 tablespoons heavy
    cream
1 egg white

Peel the mangoes and cut the flesh away from the pits. There should be about 2 cups of mango pieces. Reserve about ½ cup of the pieces and puree the remainder with the lime juice in a blender or food processor.

Add the brown sugar, the cream and egg white, and blend again to combine.

Chop the reserved mango and stir it into the mixture. Chill the mixture.

Freeze in your Donvier Ice Cream Maker according to the instructions on page 10 .

Chartreuse Ice Cream

Chartreuse has a distinctive flavor (and color), but you can substitute whatever liqueur you prefer, or have handy.

Makes about 1 pint; recipe can be doubled for about 1 quart.

1 cup milk
1 cup heavy cream
⅓ cup superfine sugar
1 teaspoon vanilla extract
2 teaspoons chartreuse liqueur

Combine the milk and cream with the sugar. Whisk for about 2 minutes, or until the sugar dissolves.

Stir in the vanilla extract, then stir in the liqueur. Chill if necessary.

Freeze in your Donvier Ice Cream Maker according to the instructions on page 10.

Ginger Ice Cream with Vodka

Ginger, vodka and cream make a triumphant troika.

Makes about 1 pint; recipe can be doubled for about 1 quart.

¼ cup finely chopped candied ginger
¼ cup vodka
¾ cup milk
¾ cup heavy cream
⅓ cup superfine sugar
1 teaspoon vanilla extract

Combine the candied ginger and the vodka and leave to soak for a few minutes.

Combine the milk and cream with the sugar. Whisk for about 2 minutes, or until the sugar dissolves.

Stir in the vanilla extract and the ginger and vodka, mixing well. Chill if necessary.

Freeze in your Donvier Ice Cream Maker according to the instructions on page 10.

Oreo Cookie Ice Cream

For the children and the Peter Pan in us all.

Makes about 1 pint; recipe can be doubled for about 1 quart.

4 Oreo cookies
¾ cup milk
¾ cup heavy cream
⅓ cup superfine sugar
1 teaspoon vanilla extract

Chop the Oreo cookies into small pieces, or crush them with a rolling pin.

Combine the milk and the cream with the sugar. Whisk for about 2 minutes, or until the sugar dissolves.

Stir in the vanilla extract and the crushed Oreo cookies. Chill if necessary.

Freeze in your Donvier Ice Cream Maker according to the instructions on page 10.

♥ LITE VERSION

For Oreo Cookie Ice Milk, substitute whole milk for the cream and low-fat milk for the milk; and you may wish to reduce the amount of sugar—but not the number of Oreo cookies!

Banana Ice Cream

Bananas do not have a season—so you can make this at any time of year.

Makes about 1 pint; recipe can be doubled for about 1 quart.

2 medium-size ripe bananas
½ cup heavy cream
¾ cup milk
⅓ cup superfine sugar
1 teaspoon vanilla extract

Puree the bananas in a blender or food processor, adding a little of the cream. You should have about 1½ cups of puree. Refrigerate.

Combine the rest of the cream and milk with the sugar. Whisk for about 2 minutes, or until the sugar dissolves.

Stir in the vanilla extract and add the banana puree, stirring well. Chill if necessary.

Freeze in your Donvier Ice Cream Maker according to the instructions on page 10.

♥ LITE VERSION

Puree the bananas with 2 cups low-fat milk, 1 teaspoon vanilla extract and 2 teaspoons lemon juice.

Aunt Alice's
Berry Cheesecake Ice Cream

Aunt Alice doesn't actually exist. We made her up, because this is the kind of thing we know she would give to us when she invited us over to visit.

Makes about 1 pint; recipe can be doubled for about 1 quart.

¾ cup milk
¾ cup heavy cream
⅓ cup and 2 table-
   spoons superfine
   sugar
1 teaspoon vanilla
   extract
8 ounces cream cheese
   (the fresh kind,
   if available)
¼ cup strawberry or
   seedless raspberry or
   blackberry preserves

Combine the milk and cream with the ⅓ cup sugar. Whisk for about 2 minutes, or until the sugar dissolves. Stir in the vanilla extract.

Beat the cream cheese with the remaining 2 tablespoons sugar until fluffy. Fold the cream cheese mixture into the milk and cream. Stir in the preserves lightly, to give a marbled effect. Chill the mixture.

Freeze in your Donvier Ice Cream Maker according to the instructions on page 10.

The classic cooked or "custard" types of ice cream are rather smoother to the taste than the simple combination of fruit, sugar and cream—and still, the custard takes only 10 minutes to cook. If you wish, add a tablespoon of white corn syrup or a lightly beaten egg white to the mixture if you plan to keep the ice cream in the freezer for a day or two. This will maintain its good, smooth consistency. ♥

French Vanilla Ice Cream

Though ice cream parlors customarily offer 10, 20 or many more flavors of ice cream, vanilla is still the all-time favorite.

Makes about 1 pint; recipe can be doubled for about 1 quart.

1 cup milk
1 cup heavy cream
3 egg yolks
⅓ cup sugar
1 teaspoon flour
3-inch piece vanilla bean or 1 teaspoon vanilla extract

Heat the milk and cream to simmering point in a saucepan.

Combine the egg yolks and sugar in a bowl and add the flour, stirring with a wire whisk. Stir the hot milk and cream into the egg mixture and return it to the saucepan. Split the vanilla bean in half lengthwise and scrape the black seeds into the mixture. Drop in the bean.

Place the saucepan over low heat and stir until the mixture thickens into a light custard. Remove from the heat and discard the vanilla bean, or stir in the vanilla extract.

Cool the mixture to room temperature, then chill approximately 1 hour in the refrigerator.

Freeze in your Donvier Ice Cream Maker according to the instructions on page 10.

Chocolate Ice Cream

Our national passion shows no signs of diminishing. With each passing moment we go on loving it more and yet more.

Makes about 1 pint; recipe can be doubled for about 1 quart.

4 ounces extra bitter-sweet chocolate or 3 ounces semi-sweet and 1 ounce unsweetened
¾ cup milk
¾ cup heavy cream
3 egg yolks
⅓ cup sugar
1 teaspoon flour
1 teaspoon vanilla extract

Melt the chocolate in a double boiler. When the water comes to a boil, remove from heat and let sit 5 minutes or until the chocolate has melted (do not cover).

Heat the milk and cream to simmering point in a saucepan.

Combine the egg yolks and sugar in a bowl and add the flour, stirring with a wire whisk. Stir the hot milk and cream into the egg mixture and return it to the saucepan. Place the saucepan over low heat and stir until the mixture thickens into a light custard. Remove from the heat.

Stir in the vanilla extract and the melted chocolate, mixing well. Cool the mixture to room temperature, then chill.

Freeze in your Donvier Ice Cream Maker according to the instructions on page 10.

♥ LITE VERSION

For Chocolate Ice Milk, substitute low-fat milk for the milk and whole milk for the cream; and reduce the amount of sugar to 1 tablespoon.

Butterscotch Ice Cream

The only thing better than serving ice cream with hot butterscotch sauce is to put the butterscotch directly into the ice cream.

Makes about 1 pint; recipe can be doubled for about 1 quart.

1 cup milk
1 cup heavy cream
3 egg yolks
⅓ cup sugar
1 teaspoon flour
1 teaspoon vanilla extract
½ cup brown sugar
2 tablespoons unsalted butter

Heat the milk and ½ cup of the cream to simmering point in a saucepan.

Combine the egg yolks and sugar in a bowl and add the flour, stirring with a wire whisk. Stir the hot milk and cream into the egg mixture and return it to the saucepan. Place the saucepan over low heat and stir until the mixture thickens into a light custard. Remove from the heat and stir in the vanilla extract.

Meanwhile, make the butterscotch by combining the brown sugar, butter and the remaining cream in a saucepan over moderate heat. Bring to the boiling point, reduce heat and simmer for about 15 minutes, stirring until smooth. Cool the butterscotch to room temperature, then add to the ice cream mixture, stirring together well. Chill the mixture.

Freeze in your Donvier Ice Cream Maker according to the instructions on page 10.

♥ LITE VERSION

For Butterscotch Ice Milk, substitute low-fat milk for the milk and whole milk for the cream; and reduce the amount of sugar to 1 tablespoon.

Maple Walnut Ice Cream

A New England specialty—though it can be enjoyed anywhere at any time.

Makes about 1 pint; recipe can be doubled for about 1 quart.

½ cup milk
½ cup heavy cream
3 egg yolks
½ cup maple syrup
1 teaspoon flour
½ cup walnuts, chopped

Heat the milk and cream to simmering point in a saucepan.

Combine the egg yolks and maple syrup in a bowl and add the flour, stirring with a wire whisk. Stir the hot milk and cream slowly into the egg mixture and return it to the saucepan. Place the saucepan over low heat and stir until the mixture thickens into a light custard. Remove from the heat.

Cool the mixture to room temperature. Stir in the chopped walnuts. Chill the mixture.

Freeze in your Donvier Ice Cream Maker according to the instructions on page 10.

Butter Pecan Ice Cream

We thought this was our absolute favorite recipe—though it turns out whichever flavor we are eating at the moment is the best of all!

Makes about 1 pint; recipe can be doubled for about 1 quart.

½ cup pecans, lightly chopped
2 tablespoons unsalted butter
¾ cup milk
¾ cup heavy cream
3 egg yolks
⅓ cup sugar
1 teaspoon flour
1 teaspoon vanilla extract

Sauté the pecan pieces in the butter, stirring, for 3-4 minutes, until they are nicely toasted. Remove from the heat and leave to cool.

Heat the milk and cream to simmering point in a saucepan.

Combine the egg yolks and sugar in a bowl and add the flour, stirring with a wire whisk. Stir the hot milk and cream into the egg mixture and return it to the saucepan. Place the saucepan over low heat and stir until the mixture thickens into a light custard. Remove from the heat.

Stir in the vanilla extract and the buttery pecan pieces. Cool the mixture to room temperature, then chill.

Freeze in your Donvier Ice Cream Maker according to the instructions on page 10.

♥ **LITE VERSION**

For Butter Pecan Ice Milk, substitute low-fat milk for the milk and whole milk for the cream; and reduce the amount of sugar to 1 tablespoon.

Praline Ice Cream

Praline is a wonderfully useful ingredient to have on hand for decorating desserts and confections. If you double the quantity needed, you can store the extra in a container with a tight-fitting lid, at room temperature.

Makes about 1 pint; recipe can be doubled for about 1 quart.

½ cup and ⅓ cup sugar, measured separately
½ cup water
½ cup skinless almonds
¾ cup milk
¾ cup heavy cream
3 egg yolks
1 teaspoon flour
1 teaspoon vanilla extract

Preheat the oven to 375 degrees. Oil a baking sheet.

Spread the almonds on foil and place in the preheated oven for 5-10 minutes, until toasted to a golden brown. Keep warm.

Meanwhile, combine the ½ cup sugar and the water in a saucepan and place over medium-high heat. Cook for about 10 minutes until a golden brown caramel syrup has formed.

Stir in the toasted almonds. Pour the caramel mixture onto the oiled baking sheet. Put the baking sheet in a cool place for the praline to set. When cool, break into pieces and pulverize in a food processor.

Meanwhile, combine the egg yolks and sugar in a bowl and add the flour, stirring with a wire whisk. Stir the hot milk and cream into the egg mixture and return it to the saucepan. Place the saucepan over low heat and stir until the mixture thickens into a light custard. Remove from the heat.

Stir in the vanilla extract. Cool the mixture to room temperature. Stir in ½ cup of the pulverized praline. Chill the mixture.

Freeze in your Donvier Ice Cream Maker according to the instructions on page 10, and serve the ice cream with the remaining crushed praline sprinkled over the top.

Raisin Chestnut Ice Cream
à la James Beard

James Beard was a man with a golden palate—this was among his favorite flavors of ice cream.

Makes about 1 pint; recipe can be doubled for about 1 quart.

¼ cup raisins
¼ cup dark rum
½ cup milk
¾ cup heavy cream
3 egg yolks
⅓ cup sugar
1 teaspoon flour
1 teaspoon vanilla extract
¼ cup chestnut puree

Put the raisins in a saucepan and pour the rum over them. Place the saucepan over moderate heat. Bring to the boiling point and remove from the heat at once. Let stand, covered, at room temperature.

Heat the milk and cream to simmering point in a saucepan.

Combine the egg yolks and sugar in a bowl and add the flour, stirring with a wire whisk. Stir the hot milk and cream into the egg mixture and return it to the saucepan. Place the saucepan over low heat and stir until the mixture thickens into a light custard. Remove from the heat .

Stir in the vanilla extract, then the chestnut puree, then the raisins and rum, mixing well. Cool the mixture to room temperature, then chill.

Freeze in your Donvier Ice Cream Maker according to the instructions on page 10 .

♥ **LITE VERSION**

For Raisin Chestnut Ice Milk, substitute low-fat milk for the milk and whole milk for the cream; and reduce the amount of sugar to 1 tablespoon.

Macadamia Nut Ice Cream à la Simca

This is an adaptation of a recipe by Simone Beck, who, with Julia Child and Louisette Bertholle, wrote the classic cookbook Mastering the Art of French Cooking.

Makes about 1 pint; recipe can be doubled for about 1 quart.

½ cup macadamia nuts
¾ cup milk
¾ cup heavy cream
3 egg yolks
⅓ cup sugar
1 teaspoon flour
1 teaspoon vanilla
   extract

Preheat the oven to 375 degrees.

Spread the macadamia nuts on foil and place in the preheated oven for about 8 minutes or until golden brown. Cool to room temperature and chop finely.

Meanwhile, heat the milk and cream to simmering point in a saucepan.

Combine the egg yolks and sugar in a bowl and add the flour, stirring with a wire whisk. Stir the hot milk and cream into the egg mixture and return it to the saucepan. Place the saucepan over low heat and stir until the mixture thickens into a light custard. Remove from the heat .

Stir in the vanilla extract and the chopped nuts. Cool the mixture to room temperature, then chill.

Freeze in your Donvier Ice Cream Maker according to the instructions on page 10.

♥ LITE VERSION

For Macadamia Nut Ice Milk, substitute low-fat milk for the milk and whole milk for the cream; and reduce the amount of sugar to 1 tablespoon.

Espresso Ice Cream à la Marcella Hazan

When the definitive author of Italian cookbooks for Americans makes her ice cream, she actually brews the espresso in her machine, using milk in place of water. This may be a trial for the espresso machine, but it's marvelous for the ice cream. Our version calls for a quick and easy way of making the espresso.

Makes about 1 pint; recipe can be doubled for about 1 quart.

1 cup milk
1 cup heavy cream
3 egg yolks
⅓ cup sugar
1 teaspoon flour
1 teaspoon vanilla
  extract
1½-2 tablespoons
  instant espresso
  powder

Heat the milk and cream to simmering point in a saucepan.

Combine the egg yolks and sugar in a bowl and add the flour, stirring with a wire whisk. Stir the hot milk and cream into the egg mixture and return it to the saucepan. Place the saucepan over low heat and stir until the mixture thickens into a light custard. Remove from the heat.

Immediately stir in the vanilla extract and the espresso powder (less or more, depending on how strong you like your espresso). Cool the mixture to room temperature, then chill.

Freeze in your Donvier Ice Cream Maker according to the instructions on page 10.

♥ **LITE VERSION**

For Espresso Ice Milk, substitute low-fat milk for the milk and whole milk for the cream; and reduce the amount of sugar to 1 tablespoon.

Sorbets,
Sherbets
& Ices

Strawberry Citrus Sorbet

A splendid sorbet, full of sparkling flavor, this may well become the specialty of your house.

Makes about 1 pint; recipe can be doubled for about 1 quart.

2 cups sliced strawberries, tightly packed
½ cup freshly squeezed orange juice
1 tablespoon fresh lemon juice

Puree the strawberries in a blender or food processor with the orange and lemon juices. Chill the mixture.

Freeze in your Donvier Ice Cream Maker according to the instructions on page 10.

Christopher Kump's Gin and Juniper Berry Sorbet

This sorbet is best served as soon as it is frozen, but the preliminary stage of preparation can be completed the night before.

Makes about 1 pint; recipe can be doubled for about 1 quart.

¾ cup sugar
1⅓ cups water
½ cup juniper berries
3 tablespoons gin

Combine the sugar, water and juniper berries in a saucepan over low heat, stirring to dissolve the sugar. Bring to the boiling point and immediately remove from the heat. Leave in a cool place at least 30 minutes, or overnight.

Strain the mixture and reserve 1 tablespoon of the berries before discarding the rest. Pour the mixture into a blender or food processor and add the gin and 1 tablespoon of berries. Blend well. Chill the mixture.

Freeze in your Donvier Ice Cream Maker according to the instructions on page 10.

Four-Fruit Sorbet à la George Blanc

George Blanc is one of the top chefs in France: When he won his third star (France's highest culinary distinction) a few years ago he was the youngest three-star chef in the country. The exquisite flavor combination of the recipe we have adapted here gives an idea of the quality of his talent.

Makes about 1 pint; recipe can be doubled for about 1 quart.

½ cup sugar
¼ cup water
8½-ounce can crushed pineapple, drained
½ very ripe banana
¼ cup fresh lemon juice
¾ cup fresh orange juice
2 teaspoons grenadine syrup

Combine the sugar and water in a saucepan over moderate heat and cook, stirring, until the sugar dissolves. Cool to room temperature.

Pour the mixture into a blender and add the other ingredients. Blend well. Chill the mixture.

Freeze in your Donvier Ice Cream Maker according to the instructions on page 10.

Kiwi Sorbet

Kiwis keep very well in the refrigerator, so if you have some on hand you can make this sorbet at the drop of a hat—and serve it in a silver bowl. For a fanciful touch, decorate it with fresh violets.

Makes about 1 pint; recipe can be doubled for about 1 quart.

6 ripe kiwi fruit
2 tablespoons sugar

Cut a thin slice from one end of each of the kiwis and peel the skin off in a spiral, using a sharp knife blade. Put the fruit in a blender with the sugar. Chill the mixture.

Freeze in your Donvier Ice Cream Maker according to the instructions on page 10.

Pear and Red Wine Sorbet

A sophisticated sorbet for a special occasion, it is at its best eaten as soon as it is frozen. The unusually large amount of alcohol prevents it from becoming very firmly frozen—and this is as it should be.

Makes about 1 pint; recipe can be doubled for about 1 quart.

1 cup sugar
2 cups red wine
Juice of ½ lemon
3 fresh pears, peeled, cored and halved, or 6 canned halves
4 tablespoons Poire William brandy

Combine the sugar, red wine and lemon juice in a saucepan and bring to the boiling point, stirring. Reduce heat and simmer for 5 minutes.

Add the pear halves to the pan and simmer for 15 minutes longer. Remove from the heat and cool to room temperature. Spoon the pears with some of the wine syrup into a blender and puree until smooth. Add the remaining wine syrup and the brandy and blend again. Chill the mixture.

Freeze in your Donvier Ice Cream Maker according to the instructions on page 10.

Cantaloupe Sorbet

It's hard to buy a perfect cantaloupe, but when I do find one that is fully ripe and exploding with luscious juicy taste, I like to transform it into a sorbet and serve it with fresh raspberries or blackberries.

Makes about 1 pint; recipe can be doubled for about 1 quart.

1 ripe medium-size cantaloupe
2 tablespoons sugar
1 tablespoon freshly squeezed lemon juice

Cut the cantaloupe into quarters lengthwise and scrape out all the seeds. Cut the ripe flesh away from the rind and cut it into pieces. Put the pieces in a food processor with the sugar and lemon juice and blend to a puree. Chill the mixture.

Freeze in your Donvier Ice Cream Maker according to the instructions on page 10.

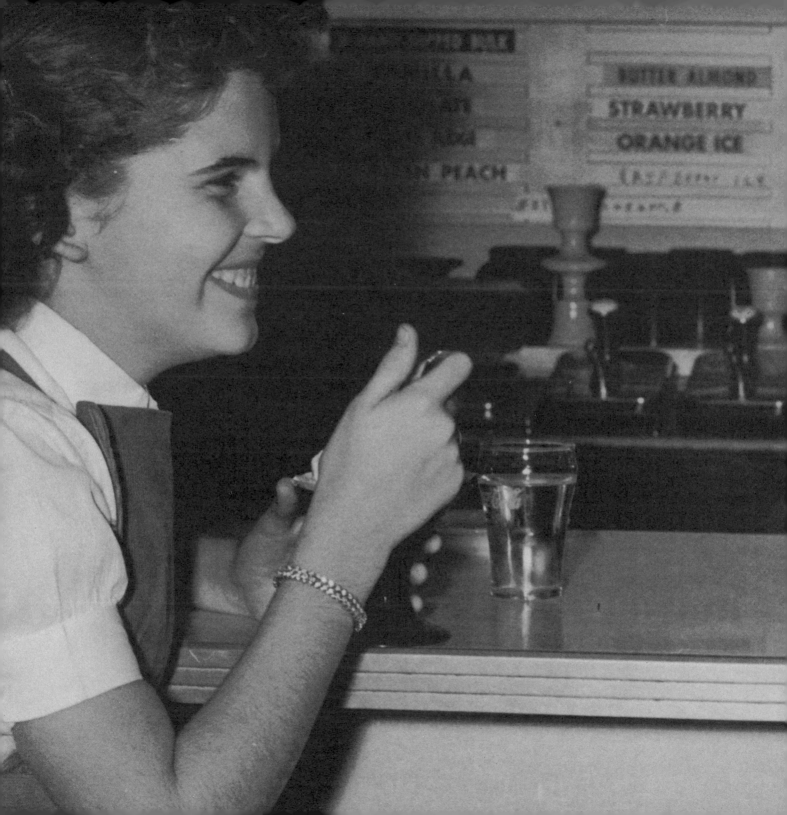

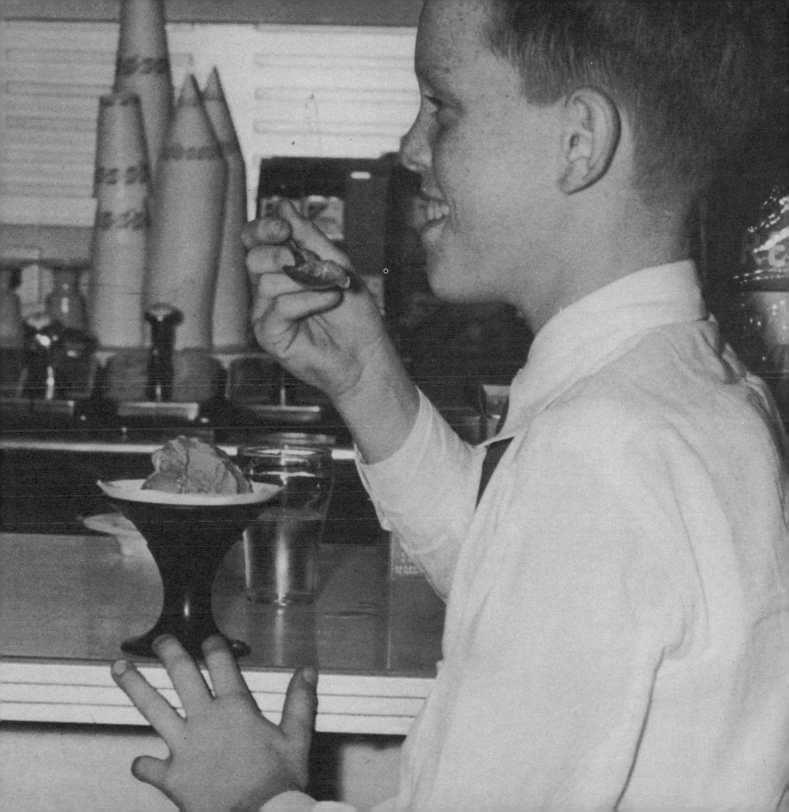

Rosa Ross's Lychee Sherbet

Despite her name, Rosa is Chinese and so comes by her inclination for lychees naturally. We added the cream to Rosa's recipe and liked the result, and we are sure you will too.

Makes about 1 pint; recipe can be doubled for about 1 quart.

20-ounce can lychees, whole, peeled, in heavy syrup
¼ cup heavy cream
1 teaspoon finely chopped lemon rind
¼ teaspoon ground cloves

Drain the lychees and pour the syrup into a measuring cup. Puree the fruit in a blender. Combine 1 cup of the pureed fruit with 1 cup of the syrup. (If the syrup is less than 1 cup, make up the difference with pureed fruit.) Add the cream, lemon rind and cloves, and mix well.

Freeze in your Donvier Ice Cream Maker according to the instructions on page 10.

Orange-Campari Sherbet

This is an idea for something really good. Now you have the idea, too, you can add any other fortified wine to this quantity of orange juice and sugar syrup, and make endless variations on the theme!

Makes about 1 pint; recipe can be doubled for about 1 quart.

⅓ cup sugar
½ cup water
1½ cups freshly squeezed orange juice
2 tablespoons Campari
1 egg white

Combine the sugar and water in a heavy-bottomed saucepan, stirring, and bring to a boil. Boil for 5 minutes, then remove from the heat and cool.

Combine the orange juice and Campari in a separate bowl. Add the sugar syrup and mix thoroughly. Beat the egg white until stiff and carefully fold into the orange juice mixture.

Chill the mixture. Freeze in your Donvier Ice Cream Maker according to the instructions on page 10.

Red Zinger Granita

This is exceptionally refreshing and can be eaten in large quantities without dismay because there is so little sugar in it—which also helps give it the grainy snow-like texture that makes a granita so appealing on a really hot day.

Makes about 1 pint; recipe can be doubled for about 1 quart.

2 bags Celestial
   Seasonings Red
   Zinger tea
2 cups boiling water
¼ cup sugar
Juice of ½ lemon

Drop the tea bags into the boiling water and let steep for 5 minutes. Remove the tea bags and add the sugar and lemon juice and stir in well to dissolve the sugar. Cool to room temperature, then chill the mixture.

Freeze in your Donvier Ice Cream Maker according to the instructions on page 10.

Lemon Granita à la James Beard

James Beard, who was usually absorbed in the main part of a meal rather than its conclusion, generally preferred fruit desserts. Of the fruits, lemon was one of his favorites.

Makes about 1 pint; recipe can be doubled for about 1 quart.

¾ cup sugar
1½ cups water
Zest of 1 lemon,
   finely chopped
½ cup fresh lemon
   juice

Combine the sugar and water in a saucepan. Bring to the boiling point, lower the heat and simmer for 5 minutes.

Remove from the heat and cool to room temperature. Stir in the chopped lemon rind and lemon juice. Chill the mixture.

Freeze in your Donvier Ice Cream Maker according to the instructions on page 10.

Chilled
& Frozen
Desserts

Margaret Paull's
Mile-High Strawberry Pie

Serves 8 (generously).

Crust:
 1 tablespoon butter
 2 tablespoons sugar
12 shortbread cookies,
   crushed to fine
   crumbs
 1 cup sliced
   strawberries
½ cup sugar
 2 egg whites
 1 teaspoon lemon juice
⅛ teaspoon salt
French Vanilla Ice Cream
   mixture (page 27),
   chilled

Combine the butter and sugar in a saucepan and cook over low heat until the sugar has melted. Mix with the cookie crumbs. Press the mixture evenly over the bottom and sides of a buttered 9-inch pie plate. Refrigerate.

Meanwhile, reserving a few berries for decoration, combine the strawberries, sugar, egg whites, lemon juice and salt in the large bowl of an electric mixer. Beat at medium speed for 15 minutes or until the mixture is stiff and holds its shape.

Freeze the chilled ice cream mixture in your Donvier Ice Cream Maker, according to the instructions on page 10, but only for 10-12 minutes; then fold the semi-soft ice cream mixture into the strawberry mixture. Spoon the strawberry cream into the pie shell, mounding it high in the center and sloping to the outer rim. Place in the freezer for several hours or overnight. Decorate with the reserved strawberries.

Frozen Lemon Torte

Serves 8.

4 teaspoons grated
  zest of lemon
⅓ cup lemon juice
French Vanilla Ice Cream
  mixture (page 27)
3 egg whites
1 cup heavy cream
2¼ cups fine vanilla
  wafer crumbs
3 tablespoons unsalted
  butter, melted

Stir the grated lemon and lemon juice into the French Vanilla Ice Cream mixture. Cool to room temperature, then chill.

Freeze in your Donvier Ice Cream Maker according to the instructions on page 10, but only for 10-12 minutes.

Beat the egg whites until stiff and fold them into the semi-soft lemon cream. Beat the remaining 1 cup of heavy cream and fold into the mixture.

Combine the vanilla wafer crumbs and the melted butter. Spoon about a third of the crumb mixture into a buttered 9-inch springform pan and press down evenly over the bottom of the pan. Gently spoon half of the lemon cream mixture on top of the crumbs and level it smoothly with a spatula. Add another third of the crumb mixture to form a third layer, working very gently. Spoon on the other half of the lemon cream as a fourth layer, and top with the remainder of the crumb mixture, smoothing the top.

Place the torte in the freezer to freeze until firm, 2 hours or longer. Unmold to serve.

Deep-Fried Ice Cream Balls

Never heard of fried ice cream? Now you have! To serve it, make a pool of your favorite ice cream sauce on each of 4 dessert plates, and keep the plates ready in the refrigerator.

Serves 8.

- 1 pint French Vanilla Ice Cream (page 27)
- ⅓ cup finely chopped almonds
- ⅔ cup dried pound-cake crumbs
- 1 egg
- 1 teaspoon sugar
- ¼ teaspoon almond extract
- **Oil for deep-frying**

Line a pie plate with plastic wrap and place in the freezer until well chilled. Form the ice cream into 4 equal balls, using an ice cream scoop, working quickly and placing each ball on the plate in the freezer as soon as formed. Leave until very firm.

Meanwhile, combine the almonds and cake crumbs, and beat the egg lightly with the sugar and almond extract.

One at a time, remove the balls from the freezer and roll in the crumb mixture, coating each one well before replacing it in the freezer. Again removing them from the freezer one at a time, dip the coated balls in the egg and sugar mixture, then roll them a second time in the crumb mixture. Return to the freezer and leave for several hours or overnight, to freeze very hard.

In a deep-fryer heat oil (at least 3 inches deep) to 375 degrees. Fry the ice cream balls for 30-40 seconds each, immediately removing them from the oil and setting them on paper towels to drain before serving.

Blueberry Maple Cream

Serves 4.

1 cup fresh blue-
  berries, or well
  drained frozen ones
4 tablespoons maple
  syrup
½ cup crème fraîche or
  sour cream

Combine the ingredients and freeze in your Donvier Ice Cream Maker according to the instructions on page 10.

Coffee Coupe

Serves 4.

1 pint firmly frozen
  Espresso Ice Cream
  (page 39)
1⅓ cups freshly brewed
  hot espresso or
  strong coffee
Crème Chantilly (page 84)

Divide the ice cream into 4 chilled parfait glasses with a scoop. Pour ⅓ cup hot coffee over the ice cream in each glass. Top with the Crème Chantilly and serve at once.

Baked Alaska

Serves 6.

1 pint French Vanilla
   Ice Cream (page 27),
   frozen 10-12 minutes
1 frozen pound cake
4 egg whites
½ cup sugar

Spoon the semi-soft ice cream into a rectangular loaf pan the same size as the frozen pound cake (or use the foil pan the cake came in if you choose) and press it down with the back of the spoon, smoothing it to make an even layer. Place in the freezer.

When the ice cream is very firm, cut the pound cake in half horizontally and place the layer of ice cream between the two halves. Place in the freezer.

Preheat the oven to 425 degrees.

Beat the egg whites in an electric mixer until they are stiff, adding the sugar a little at a time. Continue beating until the egg whites stand in firm peaks.

Take the chilled ice cream cake from the freezer and place it on a baking sheet. Working quickly, spread the meringue evenly over the top and sides of the cake, at least an inch thick. Place in the preheated oven, and leave for 2-3 minutes, until the meringue peaks are very lightly browned. Serve at once.

Brownie Ice Cream Sandwiches

Lining the pans with wax paper in this recipe makes it easier to get the brownies out of the pan cleanly. The brownies may be prepared and baked the day before, and refrigerated overnight, but the ice cream should not be taken from the freezer for the remaining steps more than an hour or two before you plan to serve the dessert.

Makes 9 squares.

1 package brownie mix
1 pint Vanilla Ice
   Cream (page 16)

Preheat the oven to 350 degrees.

Butter the bottoms of 2 8-by-8-inch baking pans. Cut 2 pieces of wax paper to the same measurement and lightly butter them. Place in the pans and sprinkle a little flour over the butter.

Prepare the brownie dough, following instructions for a fairly dense or dry result. Pour half the brownie dough into each pan and bake in the preheated oven for 20 minutes. Let cool thoroughly.

Spread the ice cream evenly over the brownie square in one pan. Remove the brownie square from the other pan, discarding the wax paper, and place on top of the ice cream. Place in the freezer for a few minutes to firm up for cutting.

Cut into 9 squares and return the pan to the freezer until a few moments before serving time.

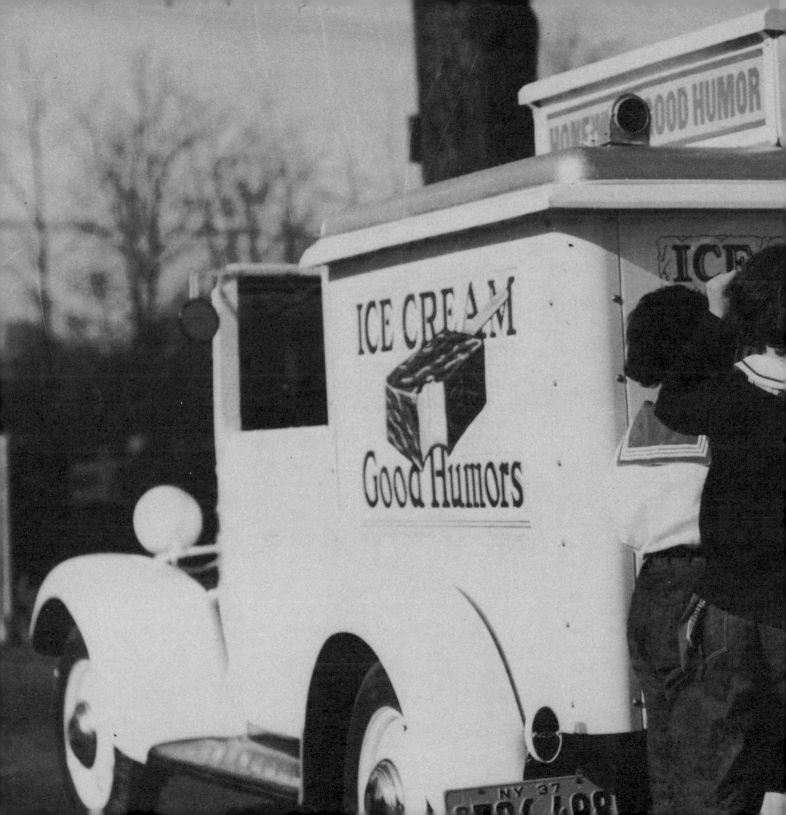

Peach Melba Bombe

Serves 6-8.

1 pint French Vanilla
 Ice Cream (page 27)
1 pint Peach Ice
 Cream (page 16)
1 cup Raspberry Sauce
 (page 89)

Line a 1-quart mold with transparent wrap so it will be easy to unmold the bombe.

Form an even layer of the vanilla ice cream all over the inside surfaces of the mold, working as quickly as possible. Place in the freezer and leave to harden for 30 minutes.

Remove from the freezer and smooth the inside of the ice cream shell in the mold. Replace in the freezer for another 15 minutes.

Fill the mold with peach ice cream, and replace in the freezer.

About an hour before you plan to serve the dessert, turn out the bombe onto a serving dish and return it to the freezer.

When ready to serve, pour a little of the Raspberry Sauce over the bombe and serve the remaining sauce separately.

Floats, Shakes, Sodas, Frappés & Frosteds

Classic Coke Float

Serve with a straw and a long-stemmed spoon.

1-2 scoops Vanilla Ice
    Cream (page 16)
 1 can Classic Coke

Drop the ice cream into a tall chilled glass. Pour in the Classic Coke.

California Root Beer Float

This drink, strictly for adults, does taste astonishingly like root beer.

Serve with a straw and a long-stemmed spoon.

 1 scoop French Vanilla
    Ice Cream (page 16)
 3 tablespoons Galliano
 2 tablespoons Kahlua
¾ cup club soda

Drop the ice cream into a tall chilled glass. Combine the Galliano, Kahlua and club soda, and pour over the ice cream.

Diet Chocolate Fudge Float

1-2 scoops Vanilla Ice
    Cream (page 16)
 1 can diet chocolate
  fudge soda

Drop the ice cream into a tall chilled glass. Pour in the diet soda.

Chocolate Milk Shake

4 tablespoons Chocolate Sauce (page 89)
1-2 scoops Vanilla Ice Cream (page 16)
1 cup cold milk

Spoon the chocolate sauce into a blender. Add the ice cream and the milk. Blend until smooth. Pour into a tall chilled glass.

Double Chocolate Milk Shake

4 tablespoons Chocolate Sauce (page 89)
1-2 scoops Chocolate Ice Cream (page 28)
1 cup cold milk

Spoon the sauce into a blender. Add the ice cream and the milk. Blend until smooth. Pour into a tall chilled glass.

Mark Gibson's Egg Nog Shake

Serves 8-10

3 egg yolks
1/3 cup sugar
2 cups milk
1/3 teaspoon vanilla extract
1/4 cup cognac
1/3 cup rum
3/4 teaspoon nutmeg
3 egg whites
1 pint French Vanilla Ice Cream (page 27)

Beat together the egg yolks and sugar. Stir the mixture into the milk. Add the vanilla extract, cognac, rum and ½ teaspoon of the nutmeg, stirring.

Beat the egg whites until stiff, and fold into the milk mixture.

Spoon the ice cream into a blender and add the mixture. Blend until smooth. Pour immediately into chilled glass punch cups and serve with the rest of the nutmeg sprinkled on top.

Strawberry Blonde Soda

Serve with a straw and a
long-stemmed spoon.

1-2 scoops Strawberry
   Ice Cream (page 17)
¼ cup cold milk
 4 tablespoons
    strawberry syrup
 1 can ginger ale

Drop the ice cream into a tall chilled glass. Pour in the cold milk and the syrup.
Fill the glass with ginger ale.

Brown Cow Soda

Serve with a straw and a
long-stemmed spoon.

 4 tablespoons Chocolate
    Sauce (page 89)
1-2 scoops Vanilla Ice
    Cream (page 16)
¼ cup cold milk
 1 cup (approximately)
    very cold root beer

Pour the chocolate sauce into a tall chilled glass. Add the ice cream, then pour in
the milk. Fill the glass with root beer.

Butterscotch Soda

Serve with a straw and a long-stemmed spoon.

1-2 scoops Vanilla Ice
    Cream (page 16)
¼ cup cold milk
4 tablespoons
    Butterscotch Sauce
    (page 85)
1 can club soda

Drop the ice cream into a tall chilled glass. Pour in the cold milk and the butterscotch sauce. Fill the glass with the club soda.

Black and White Coffee Frappé

2 scoops Espresso Ice
    Cream (page 39)
1 cup cold milk

Put the ice cream and milk in a blender and blend until smooth. Pour into a tall chilled glass.

White and Black Coffee Frappé

2 scoops Vanilla Ice
    Cream (page 16)
1 cup cold black
    coffee, sweetened
    to taste

Put the ice cream and coffee in a blender and blend until smooth. Pour into a tall chilled glass.

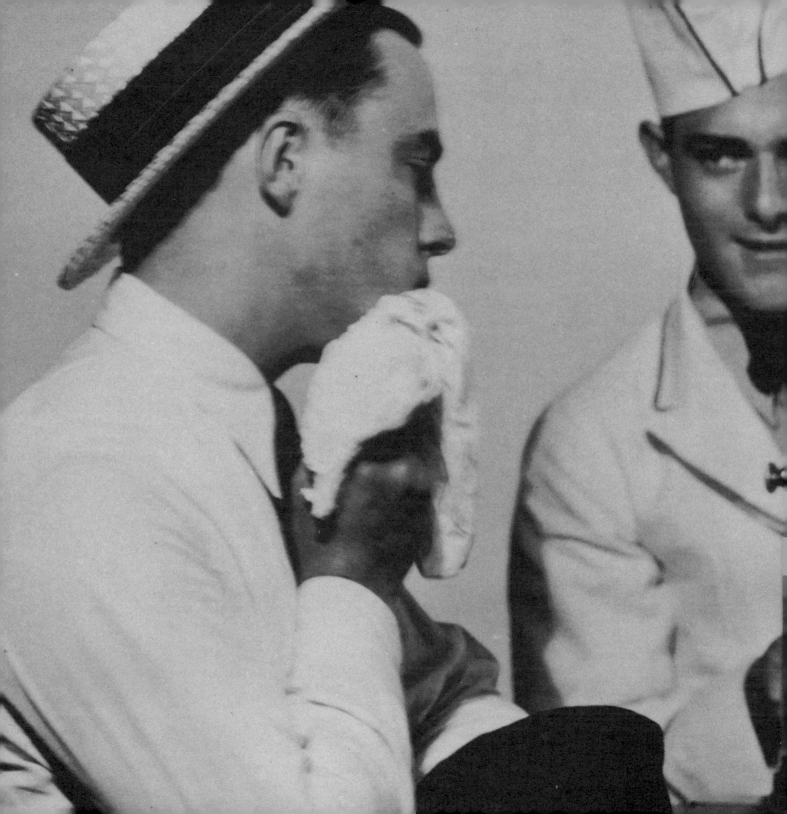

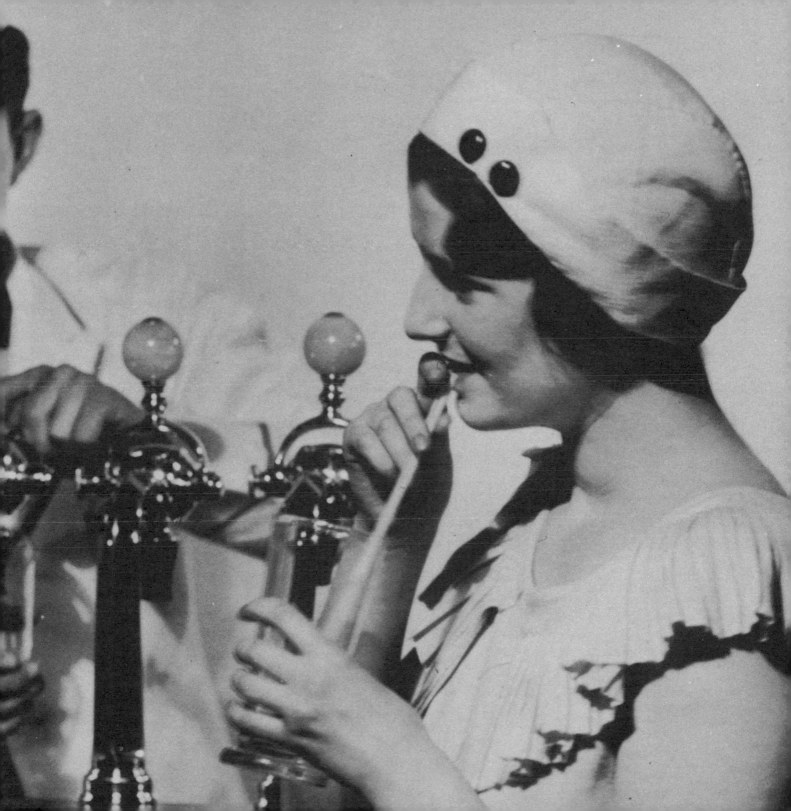

Banana Frappé

1-2 scoops Banana Ice
Cream (page 24)
1 cup cold milk

Put the ice cream in a blender and add the milk. Blend until smooth. Pour into a tall chilled glass.

Caramel Frosted

4 tablespoons Caramel
Sauce (page 84)
1-2 scoops French
Vanilla Ice Cream
(page 27)
1 can club soda

Spoon the sauce into a blender and add the ice cream and club soda. Blend until smooth. Pour into a tall chilled glass.

Chocolate Sprite Frosted

3 tablespoons Choco-
late Sauce (page 89)
1-2 scoops Vanilla Ice
Cream (page 16)
1 can Sprite

Spoon the sauce into a blender. Add the ice cream and the Sprite and blend until smooth. Pour into a tall chilled glass.

Orange Dreamsicle Frosted

The frozen confection on a stick which is orange ice surrounding a core of vanilla ice cream has long been known as an Orange Creamsicle in many parts of America, but to Texans they have always been and always will be Dreamsicles.

1-2 scoops French
   Vanilla Ice Cream
   (page 27)
 1 can Orange Slice

Combine the ice cream and Orange Slice in a blender and blend until smooth. Pour into a tall chilled glass.

Raspberry Frosted

3 tablespoons
   Raspberry Sauce
   (page 89)
1-2 scoops Vanilla Ice
   Cream (page 16)
 1 can ginger ale

Spoon the raspberry sauce into a blender, and add the ice cream and ginger ale. Blend until smooth. Pour into a tall chilled glass.

Frozen Drinks

Brandy Freeze

Serves 4.

¼ cup sugar
¼ cup water
½ cup brandy
¼ cup Crème de Cacao
½ cup milk
 1 cup heavy cream

Combine the sugar and water in a saucepan over moderate heat and cook, stirring, until the sugar dissolves. Cool to room temperature.

Stir in the brandy, Crème de Cacao, milk and cream.

Partially freeze in your Donvier Ice Cream Maker according to the instructions on page 10, but for only half the freezing time. Pour or spoon the semi-frozen mixture into chilled glasses.

Frozen Margaritas

Serves 4.

½ cup gold Tequila
½ cup Cointreau
½ cup lime juice
½ cup water
Fresh lime wedge
Coarse salt

Combine the Tequila, Cointreau, lime juice and water.

Partially freeze in your Donvier Ice Cream Maker according to the instructions on page 10, but for only half the freezing time.

Meanwhile rub the rims of 4 chilled stemmed glasses with the lime wedge, then dip in salt. Chill the glasses until ready to serve.

Spoon or pour the semi-frozen mixture into the glasses when ready to serve.

Frozen Mimosas

Serves 4.

¾ cup freshly squeezed
   orange juice
1¼ cups champagne
 4 fresh strawberries

Combine the orange juice and champagne.

Partially freeze in your Donvier Ice Cream Maker according to the instructions on page 10, but for only half the freezing time.

Put a strawberry in each of 4 stemmed glasses and put in the freezer to chill.

Pour or spoon the semi-frozen mixture over the strawberries in the chilled glasses when ready to serve.

Richie's Strawberry Daiquiri

Serves 4.

1 cup fresh straw-
   berries, sliced and
   tightly packed
Juice of 1 lemon
Juice of 1 lime
½ cup rum
¼ cup water
3 tablespoons
   grenadine syrup

Puree all the ingredients in a blender or food processor.

Partially freeze the mixture in your Donvier Ice Cream Maker according to the instructions on page 10, but for only half the freezing time. Pour or spoon the semi-frozen mixture into chilled glasses and serve at once.

Frozen Bellinis

Serves 4.

8 ounces canned
   peaches packed in
   syrup (half a 16-
   ounce can)
1 tablespoon freshly
   squeezed lemon
   juice
1½ cups champagne

Drain the peaches, saving the syrup, and chop them coarsely.

Measure the syrup and if less than ⅓ cup, make it up with water. Combine with the peaches, lemon juice and champagne.

Partially freeze in your Donvier Ice Cream Maker according to the instructions on page 10, but for only half the freezing time. Pour or spoon the semi-frozen mixture into chilled stemmed glasses to serve.

Sundae
Sauces &
Toppings

Marshmallow Sauce

Makes 1½ cups.

½ cup sugar
1 teaspoon corn syrup
¼ cup milk
½ teaspoon vanilla
   extract
¼ pound (or 15 large)
   marshmallows
1 tablespoon water

Combine the sugar, corn syrup and milk in a saucepan and simmer gently, stirring, for 5 minutes. Remove from the heat and stir in the vanilla extract.

Put the marshmallows and water in the top of a double boiler and heat over boiling water until melted, stirring occasionally.

Stir the sugar mixture over the melted marshmallow and stir until well combined.

Serve warm or cooled to room temperature; in the latter case it will benefit from being beaten just before serving.

Crème Chantilly

Makes 1 cup.

1 cup heavy cream
1 tablespoon confec-
   tioners' sugar
1 teaspoon vanilla
   extract

Whip the cream until thickened but not stiff, adding the sugar and vanilla extract as you whip. Refrigerate until ready to serve.

Caramel Sauce

Makes 1½ cups.

2 cups sugar
⅔ cup water
2 teaspoons lemon
   juice
1 cup heavy cream

Combine the sugar, water and lemon juice in a saucepan over moderate heat and cook for 10-15 minutes, until the mixture has thickened and turned golden.

Add ½ cup of the cream and cook, stirring, for 1 minute, until the foaming subsides. Add the remaining cream and stir well to incorporate. Serve warm or cooled to room temperature.

Walnut-Chocolate Sauce à la Maida Heatter

Makes 1½ cups.

3 tablespoons sugar
2 tablespoons light
   cream
½ ounce semi-sweet
   chocolate, chopped
½ ounce unsweetened
   chocolate, chopped
1 egg yolk
3 tablespoons butter
½ teaspoon vanilla
   extract
¼ cup chopped walnuts

Combine the sugar and cream in a saucepan over moderate heat and cook, stirring, until the sugar dissolves. Bring quickly to the boiling point, add the chopped chocolate and immediately remove from the heat.

Whisk quickly until the chocolate is incorporated. Add the egg yolk and whisk again.

Put the saucepan over low heat. Add the butter and whisk in. Stir in the vanilla extract and the walnuts. Serve warm or at room temperature.

Butterscotch Sauce

Makes 1 cup.

¾ cup dark brown
   sugar
4 tablespoons unsalted
   butter
¼ cup heavy cream

Combine the ingredients in a saucepan over moderate heat, stirring to mix well. Let simmer gently for about 15 minutes, and serve either warm or at room temperature.

Apricot Sauce

Makes 1 cup.

13-ounce jar apricot
   preserves
1 tablespoon Kirsch

Combine the preserves and Kirsch in a saucepan and heat, stirring, until it becomes more liquid. Press through a sieve or puree in a blender.

Chocolate Sauce

Makes 1 cup.

1 ounce unsweetened
 chocolate
4 ounces semi-sweet
 chocolate
¾ cup heavy cream

Chop all the chocolate into small pieces and add to the heavy cream in a saucepan set over low heat. Stir until the chocolate has melted.

Hot Fudge Sauce

Makes 1 cup.

2 ounces semi-sweet
 chocolate
1 ounce bittersweet
 chocolate
2 tablespoons butter
¾ cup heavy cream
¼ cup corn syrup
1 cup sugar
2 teaspoons vanilla
 extract

Chop all the chocolate into small pieces and place in a saucepan. Add the butter and cream and set over moderate heat, stirring until the chocolate has melted. Add the corn syrup and sugar and mix well, stirring, until simmering. Simmer gently, uncovered, for 15 minutes, until thickened.

Remove from the heat and stir in the vanilla extract. Serve at once or keep warm in the top of a double boiler until ready to serve.

Raspberry Sauce

This recipe will work equally well with strawberries.

Makes 1 cup.

10-ounce package frozen
 raspberries packed in
 syrup, thawed
2 tablespoons sugar
1 tablespoon Kirsch or
 Framboise, optional
1 teaspoon lemon juice

Puree all the ingredients in a blender or food processor. Press the puree through a sieve to remove the seeds.

Sundae Suggestions

Toppings To Try

Espresso Ice Cream (page 39) with Hot Fudge Sauce topped with oatmeal cookie crumbs

Macadamia Nut Ice Cream (page 38) with Raspberry Sauce topped with toasted chopped macadamia nuts

Oreo Cookie Ice Cream (page 24) with Marshmallow Sauce topped with crumbled Oreo cookies

Banana Ice Cream (page 24) with Apricot Sauce topped with crushed Heath bar crumbs

Butterscotch Ice Cream (page 29) with Butterscotch Sauce topped with toasted coconut

Peach Ice Cream (page 16) with Raspberry Sauce topped with raspberries

Strawberry Ice Cream (page 17) with Apricot Sauce topped with strawberry slices

Chocolate Peppermint Ice Cream (page 18) with Chocolate Sauce topped with crushed peppermint candies

Chocolate Ice Cream (page 28) with Marshmallow Sauce topped with chocolate sprinkles

Crumbled granola

M&Ms

Crushed Oreo cookies

Raisins

Chocolate-covered raisins

Chopped and toasted nuts, particularly macadamias

Toasted coconut shreds

Crushed Heath bars

Chocolate sprinkles

Crushed oatmeal cookies

Miniature marshmallows

Reese's peanut butter cups, frozen and then chopped

Crushed peppermint candies

Raspberries or sliced strawberries

Recipe Index

Photograph Credits

American Heritage-Horizon:
1; 4-5; 45; 92-93 courtesy of Kansas Historical Society, Topeka
Culver Pictures, Inc.:
9; 14; 22-23; 26; 50; 54-55; 65; 78; 86-87
Frederick Lewis, Inc.:
6; 19; 40; 46-47; 59 and back cover ; 88
H. Armstrong Roberts, Inc.:
11; 30-31; 33; 34-35; 60; 62-63; 66; 70-71; 74-75; 82

ALL PRODUCTS BROUGHT TO YOU BY DONVIER

Donvier, quart
Donvier, pint
Includes free color recipe book
and scoop

Extra cylinder, pint
Extra cylinder, quart

CHILDREN'S GIFTS

''Snoopy'', pint
''Penguin'', pint
½ pint

Parfait Set
4 dishes and 4 spoons per set

Sherbet Set
4 dishes and 4 spoons per set

Scoop

Donvier Diet Shakemaker

Viva Compact
Electric Ice Cream Maker